10 EXCUSES FOR WORK AVOIDANCE

Kevin, thought this may be of help to you! love as always

Anne xxx

By Mathew *Court*
& Dave *Brady*

AN ESSENTIAL GUIDE TO HOW THIS BOOK WILL WORK FOR YOU

This booklet is a guide for the employee to further their skills by providing unbelievably believable excuses to avoid work.

Ranging from the simple to the sublime these tried and tested acts of idleness will convert even the hardest of managers into cooing sympathisers.

Whether you want an excuse for being late, a couple of hours off, or the whole day to yourself, this list provides the ideal dodge for whatever your need.

Simply follow the five easy steps to that well earned rest:

STEP ONE
Prepare yourself with an excuse of your choice and rehearse the story thoroughly, until even you believe it.

STEP TWO
Be positive in saying *"I am going to be late"*, *"I feel really awful"* and *"I can't come in today"*. There will be less doubt if you are very assertive.

STEP THREE
Make that all important phone call as early as possible before the place of work is full.

STEP FOUR
Mission successful, return to your bedroom for that well deserved relaxation.

STEP FIVE
Above all, do not feel guilty and really enjoy your extra free-time.

GOOD LUCK!

What tone of voice should I adopt?

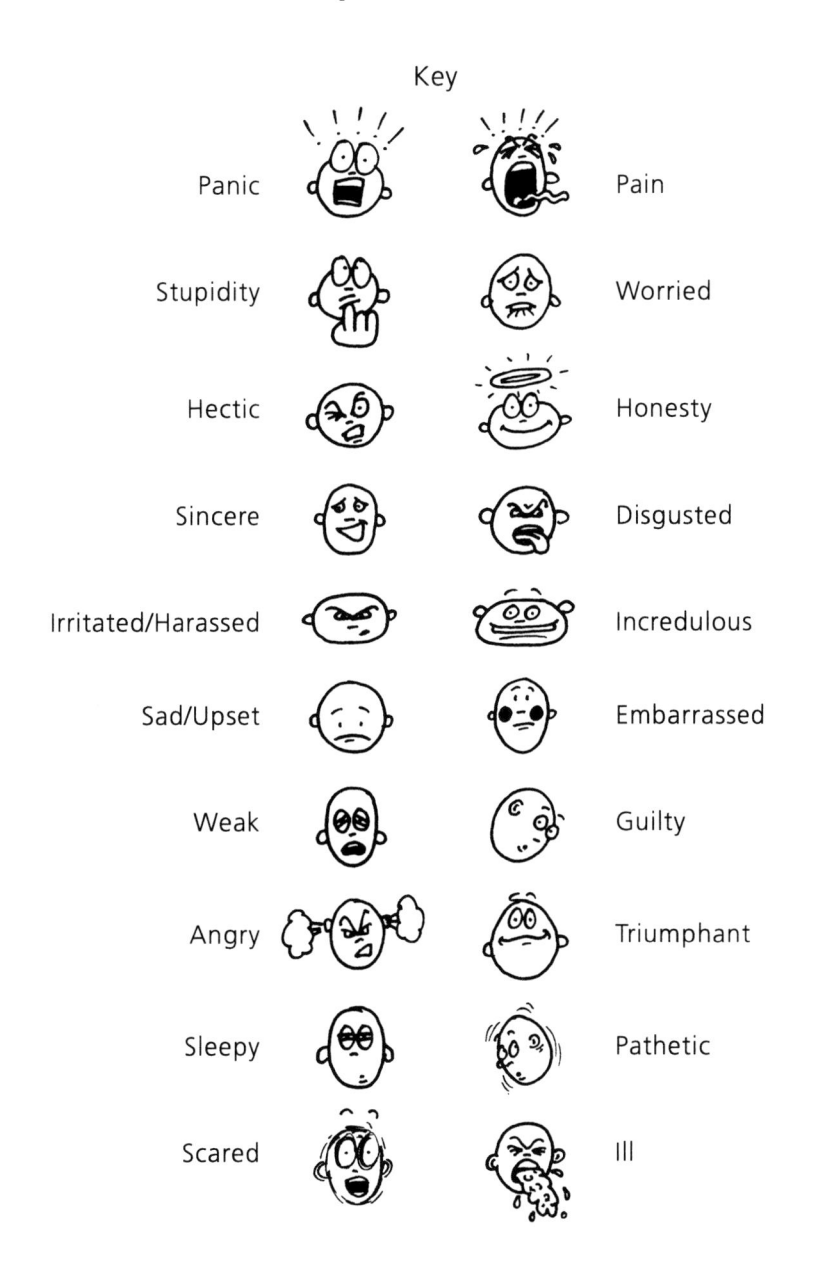

Key

Panic			Pain
Stupidity			Worried
Hectic			Honesty
Sincere			Disgusted
Irritated/Harassed			Incredulous
Sad/Upset			Embarrassed
Weak			Guilty
Angry			Triumphant
Sleepy			Pathetic
Scared			Ill

PART ONE
LATENESS

Bird shit in hair

The foul mouthed act

Ask colleagues to look into mouth to see emergency filling, show them an old one and invariably they will turn away in disgust.

Cavity oddity

Take sharp intake of breath through pursed lips and quickly touch cheek with fingertips.

Ancient pigmy tribe think I'm God

Caught cock in zip

Guaranteed sympathy from even the coldest of bosses.

Washing machine flood

Place hands in hot soapy water and leave until wrinkled.

Waiting for toothpaste to thaw

Seasonal : This one's tried and tested.

Had to give mouth to mouth on the way to work

Rushed to hospital with suspected halitosis

Phone up and speak to someone who doesn't know what it means.

Bike puncture

A couple of streaks of oil on the back of each hand and produce the offending nail.

Allergic sneezing

Before phoning, snort half a teaspoon of pepper up chosen nasal passage. (White is best)

Stiff neck

Gradually remove ear from shoulder throughout remainder of day.

You've shit yourself

Uuaargh!

Hoover blew up

The festering boil

Flinch and gasp when moving alleged area.

Lost keys

Harp on about expensive locksmiths.

Stuck in tree rescuing cat

A small sprig of foliage protruding from your attire and a nasty cat scratch will suffice. Non-cat owners use an hors d'oeuvres fork.

Swallowed toothbrush

Foul chuffs

Drink juice of one tin of marrowfat peas and consume three pickled eggs. An authentic olfactory recipe.

Re-do haircut

Make sure everyone knows your hair is being cut that evening. Call in the morning with regrettable news.

Had a fight with a commuter

Toothache

PAGE *eighteen*

The laceration
Affix sizeable dressing to limb or digit.

Doctor's visit
Elaborate about a mad old woman in the waiting room.

Locked out of house
See lost keys (**PAGE** *fifteen*) and add the cost of glaziers.

Morning sickness

Accident resulting in purchasing new clothes

Excuses range from vicious dogs to careless binmen.

Slipped in bath

You will need an old bandage, a safety pin and ketchup.

Ticket Fraud

The puddle
Water, splash it all over.

Neighbour's snake on the loose
Read up about your chosen reptile and bore your colleagues. They'll soon forget you were late.

Train's late
Signals, tunnels, leaves, commuters on the line. This one's a winner.

PAGE *twenty* three

Traffic jam

PAGE *twenty five*

PART TWO
HALF DAYS

Pet seizure

The huey dodge

Take a thermos flask containing a mixture of warm milk, wheat biscuit cereal, diced carrots and custard powder into work. Take a mouthful and blurt out noisily in front of the boss.

Severe woodworm discovery

Stopped runaway car

Substantially scuff the soles of your shoes and show off proudly to workmates.

Non specific urethritis

Make little groans before and after nature calls.

Burned ear with iron

Rub ear vigourously before entering work.

Eye infection

Rub eyes and sharply pluck nostril hairs before entering workplace.

Maggot infestation

Wretch and cough extravagantly when phoning work.

Victim of road rage

Arm in plaster
Requires allegiance with friendly nurse.

Calcium deficiency
Limp.

Partner shredded entire wardrobe

Bunged up

Pinch fleshy part of nose when speaking and suck air quickly with tongue loosely in roof of mouth.

Got covered in paint

The motor blag

Simply apply oil underneath the fingernails and smear a small amount of grime onto cheek. Pretend not to notice.

Osteopath appointment

Explain in noisy detail the bone-crunching experience.

Gout playing up

A boozy aroma, red wine nose and unhealthy waddle are essential.

Got mugged

The chimney sweepstake

Apply soot to inner ear.

Collect relative from airport

Show off the tacky holiday souvenir your tight fisted auntie brought you from Spain.

Amazing T.V. interview

Moan about cheesy media people when you get back to office.

Witnessed accident

Exploding boiler

Use cigarette lighter gas instead of deodorant that morning.

Blood test

Hold arm painfully and apply dot of red felt tip to inside of elbow.

New lease

Moan about greedy landlords, estate agents and property developers.

Tied up all kinky

Give yourself chinese burns on wrists.

Waiting for the doctor to come

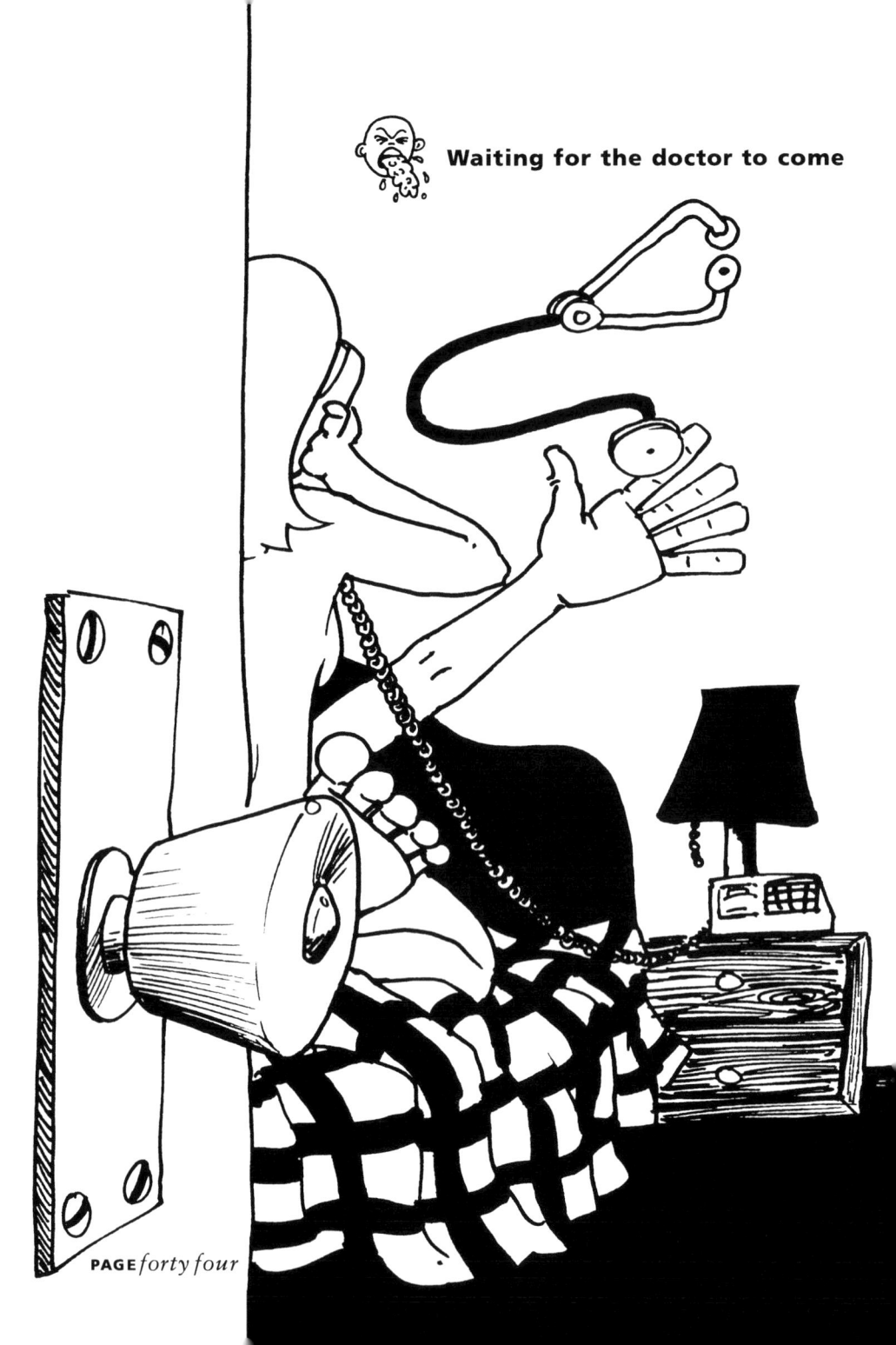

Superglued

Rub fingertips on sandpaper for authenticity.

Consoling

After taking any phone call, jump up and run out of the office muttering, *"Oh my God, oh my God."* Explain later.

The golfing incident
Wince whenever you sit down.

Lost wallet and credit card

Borrow some cash off your boss anyway.

Attic leakage

Get to work before your hair dries.

Front door replacement

See **PAGES** *fifteen* and *nineteen* and add the cost of chippies.

Squashed knackers

Finally, a chance to walk like John Wayne.

Period pain

PART THREE
ONE DAY
PLUS

Got a terrible fever

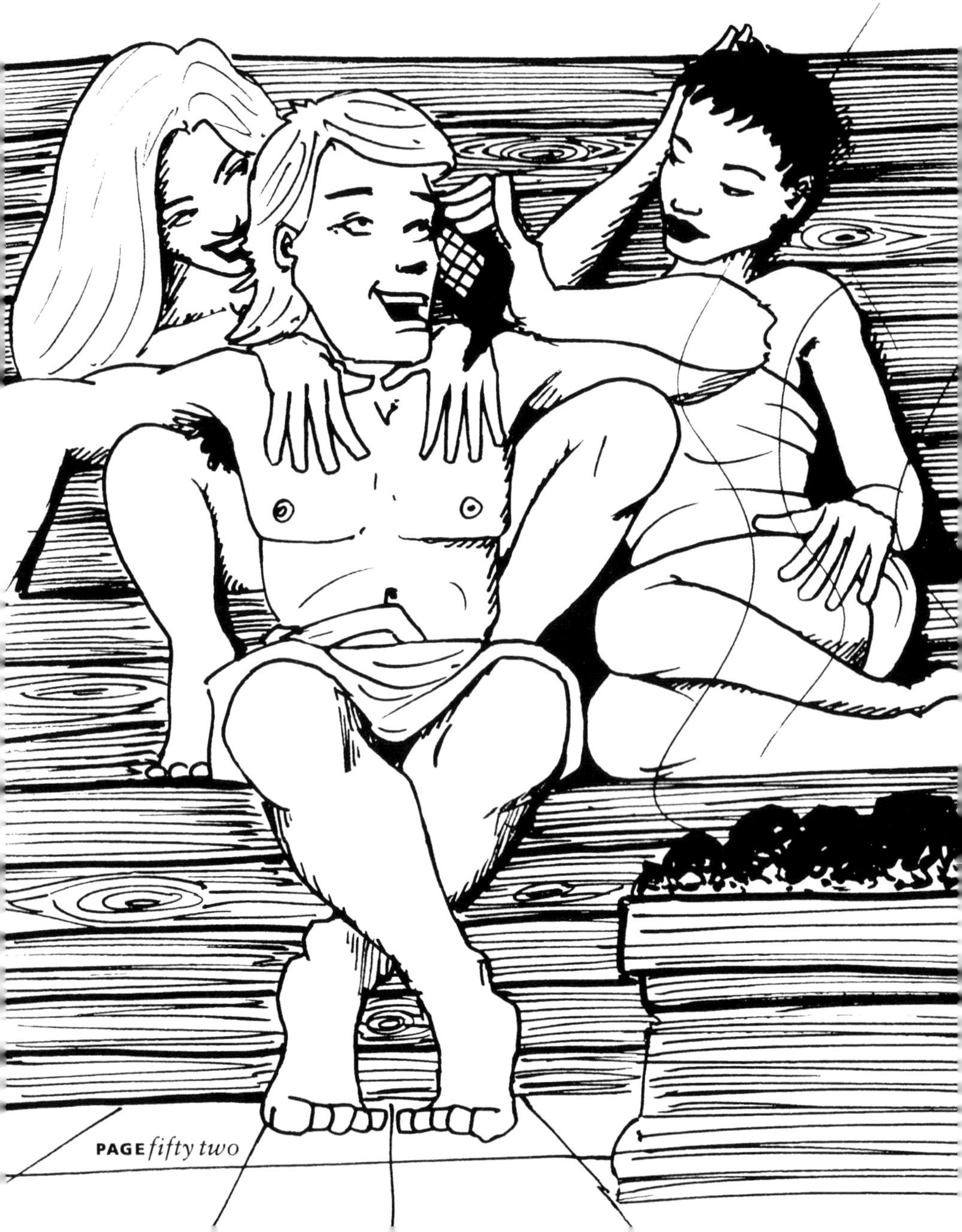

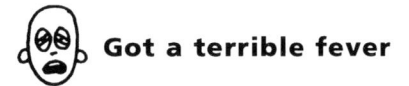

Influenza
Feign illness the day before and call with substantial grip on larynx.

Still high on drugs

Nasty illness

Scurvy, typhoid, rickets, diptheria, cholera, yellow fever, hepatitis A, polio and beri beri.

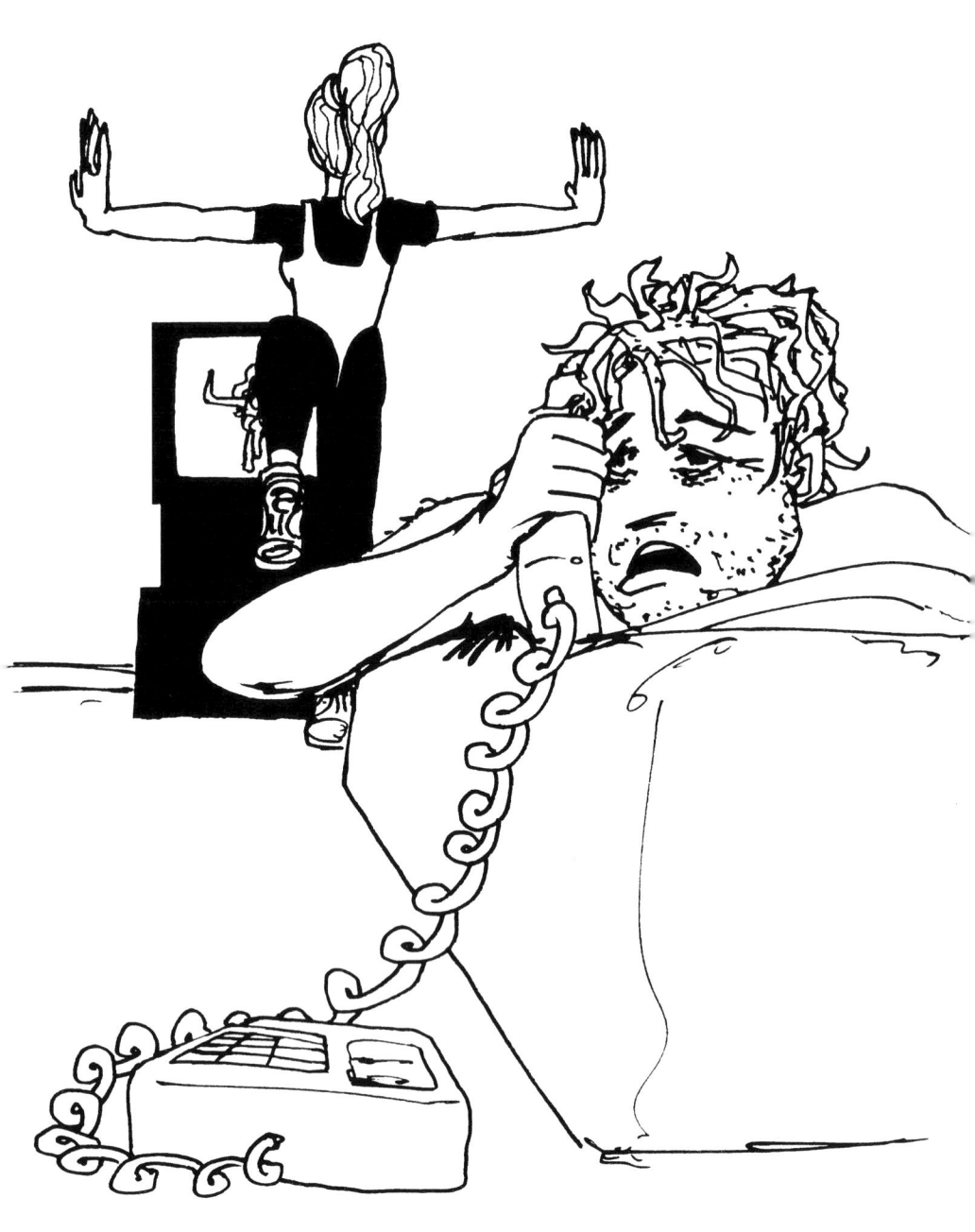

Ruptured privates

The will reading

Make up a solicitors company in a far away town and exuse yourself mournfully.

Whiplash

Broken toe

Limp painfully for several days on left foot.

Migraine

Stowaway

Enter workplace drinking from a coconut with torn trouser bottoms and shirt cuffs.

Eyebrows shaved off

If you want to do it, you've got to do it.

Bum trouble

This incorporates haemorrhoids, diarrhoea, gastroenteritis and medieval botulism.

The common complaint

Mumps, German measles, chicken pox etc.

Struck by clay pigeon

Avalanche/Mudslide

Must involve perilous route to work.

Champagne cork in eye

The burnt tongue

Talk with tongue loosely between teeth.

Got beaten up

A wedding

Sprinkle confetti around your work area.

Fell off horse

Forget people's names and simple tasks for a few days.

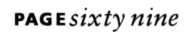

Earache

The squashed finger

Twitch little finger erratically all the next day.

Out on a stag night

Heirloom auction

Bastard uncle Bertie lied about that Rembrandt.

Sunstroke

See fell off horse (**PAGE** *sixty nine*).

Postman had a cardiac arrest

Hypothermia

Next day. While shivering, hug workmates for warmth.

A death in the family

Court witness

Pick a trial, any trial....

DIY disaster

Apply suitable dressing to relevant area.

Nan moving house

Stay off tea for a week.

Plague of nits

Sprinkle shoulders with sugar upon your return for that authentic loose scalp look.

Taken hostage by religious fundamentalists

Amnesia

Call up next day and explain.

Fire in house

Writer's cramp

PAGE *eighty five*

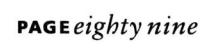

PAGE *ninety three*

PAGE *ninety five*

© July 1997 ISBN 0 9531725 0 3
Mathew Court & Dave Brady   A Mustard publication

Printed and bound in the UK by   All rights reserved. No Part of this publication
B&D Print Services Ltd.   may be reproduced, stored in a retrieval system
Rawcliffe House,   or transmitted in any form or by any means,
Marathon Place, Moss Side,   electronic, mechanical, photocopying, recording
Leyland Lancashire,   or otherwise without prior permission in writing
PR5 3QN.   from the copyright owners.